W9-CRO-204

What Can We Do About
NUCLEAR WASTE?

David J. Jakubiak

PowerKiDS
press

New York

For Alyssa Kuehn, whose discovery and commitment has inspired us all

Published in 2012 by The Rosen Publishing Group, Inc.
29 East 21st Street, New York, NY 10010

First Edition

Editor: Amelie von Zumbusch
Book Design: Kate Laczynski
Layout Design: Julio Gil

Photo Credits: Cover Matthew McVay/Stone/Getty Images; pp. 4, 6, 8 (main), 14 Shutterstock.com; p. 8 (inset) Harry Taylor/Dorling Kindersley/Getty Images; p. 10 Bradley C. Bower/Bloomberg via Getty Images; p. 12 Michael Dunning/Getty Images; p. 16 Steve Allen/Brand X Pictures/Getty Images; p. 18 David McNew/Getty Images; p. 20 John Giustina/Taxi/Getty Images.

Library of Congress Cataloging-in-Publication Data

Jakubiak, David J.
  What can we do about nuclear waste? / by David J. Jakubiak. — 1st ed.
      p. cm. — (Protecting our planet)
  Includes index.
  ISBN 978-1-4488-4983-3 (library binding) — ISBN 978-1-4488-5114-0 (pbk.) —
  ISBN 978-1-4488-5115-7 (6-pack)
  1. Radioactive wastes—Juvenile literature. 2. Nuclear engineering—Juvenile literature. I. Title.
  TD898.J35 2012
  363.72'89—dc22

                              2010052216

Manufactured in the United States of America

CPSIA Compliance Information: Batch #WS11PK: For Further Information contact Rosen Publishing, New York, New York at 1-800-237-9932

CONTENTS

Much nuclear waste comes from nuclear power plants, such as this one in

What Is Nuclear Waste?

Everything around us is made up of tiny pieces called **atoms**. Even our bodies are made of atoms. Atoms are made of even smaller bits of matter called protons, neutrons, and electrons. The neutrons and protons are in an atom's **nucleus**, or center. It takes lots of energy to hold them together there. This energy is called nuclear energy. Scientists have found ways to release and use nuclear energy.

However, releasing nuclear energy produces nuclear waste. This leftover matter is **radioactive**. This means it leaks energy. Nuclear waste can hurt living things. Therefore, it must be stored carefully.

CAUTION

RADIOACTIVE
MATERIALS

Places with radioactivity are unsafe. For this reason, they are often fenced off and marked with the yellow and black sign seen here.

Radioactivity and Living Things

There is some natural radioactivity in our bodies. Part of it comes from the food we eat. Bananas are one kind of food that is a little radioactive. Amounts of radioactivity as small as that found in bananas do not hurt us.

However, large amounts of radioactivity can hurt people and animals. People who get too close to radioactive matter can get burned. The sickness **cancer** can be caused by radiation.

Radiation can cause birth defects, too. These are changes to people's bodies that happen before they are born. Radiation can cause birth defects in animals, too.

DID YOU KNOW?

In 1986, a fire at the Chernobyl nuclear plant, in what is now Ukraine, let radioactive waste out into the air. People in the plant died. Many people who lived nearby got sick.

People dig rocks with uranium in them out of mines, such as this one in Australia. Inset: Uraninite rocks have uranium in them.

Breaking Atoms Apart

Scientists release nuclear energy by breaking certain atoms apart. The atoms that are best for this are certain **isotopes** of certain **elements**. Elements are basic kinds of matter. Isotopes are versions of one element with different numbers of neutrons. To release nuclear energy, scientists put atoms of an isotope into a **nuclear reactor**. There, they fire neutrons at it. Pieces of the isotope's atoms fly apart, hit other atoms, and break them apart. Lots of energy is released.

The isotope that scientists most often use is U-235. This is **uranium** with 143 neutrons. Its atoms are easier to break apart than those of most matter.

Nuclear plants, such as this one in Limerick, Pennsylvania, have carefully trained people who make sure the plant is running safely.

Nuclear power plants use the energy released from breaking atoms to make **electricity**. Most of the energy released when atoms break apart is in the form of heat.

In a nuclear power plant, this heat is used to boil water. This makes steam. The steam rises and turns a fan on a machine that produces electricity.

After the electricity is made, there is nuclear waste left in the reactor. All the radioactive waste that comes from making electricity for one person for 20 years would fit in a soda can. However, even this small amount of nuclear waste can release radioactivity for thousands of years.

SERIAL NO. 9B-31772 SB

Nuclear missiles are weapons that can be fired at an enemy. They are often stored in deep underground silos, such as the one seen here.

Nuclear Weapons

Some countries have used nuclear energy to make **nuclear weapons**. Nuclear weapons are powerful arms. Some nuclear weapons use the heat of atoms breaking apart. Others depend on the energy created by joining atoms together. These are the most powerful nuclear weapons. All nuclear weapons can cause horrible destruction. One nuclear weapon can flatten many buildings and kill thousands of people.

When they go off, nuclear weapons leave behind radioactive waste, called fallout. It can last for years. People who survive when a nuclear weapon hits may get sick from radiation years later.

DID YOU KNOW?

In 1945, the United States dropped two atomic bombs on Japan. It is the only time that nuclear weapons were used in a war. The countries were fighting in World War II.

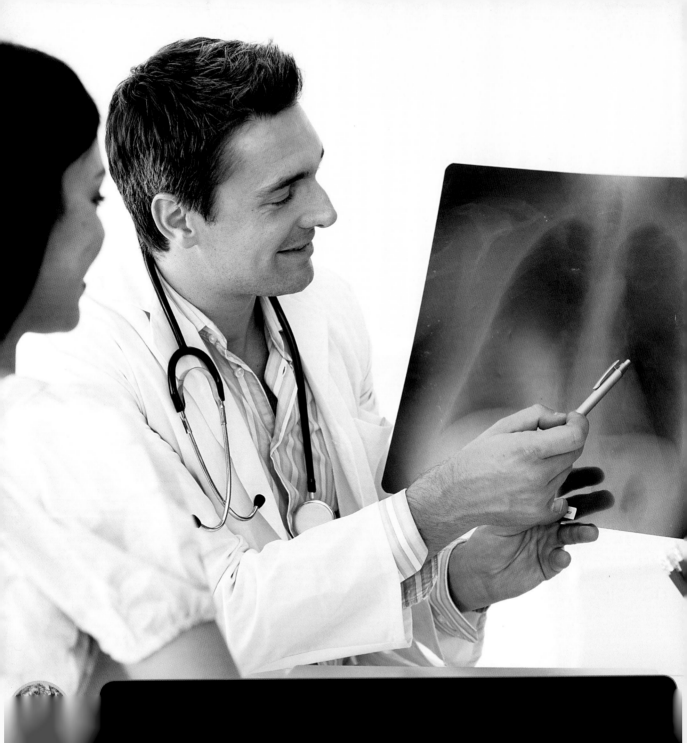

Nuclear Medicine

Doctors use radioactivity to help sick people. For example, people with cancer may get small doses of radiation. This can control the sick body cells that cause cancer.

One branch of medicine that uses radioactive materials is radiology. Using X-rays to take pictures of broken bones is one example of this.

Doctors also use isotopes of certain elements to understand why people are sick. A person eats or gets a shot of the isotope. The isotope's atoms gather around the sick parts of the person's body. Special cameras show where the isotopes are glowing. The root of the sickness has been found!

This is a nuclear reprocessing plant. In these plants, radioactive waste is separated from other waste made by a nuclear plant.

Can We Recycle Nuclear Waste?

Nuclear power plants, weapons, and medicine all make nuclear waste. Nuclear waste's radioactivity fades away over time. However, this can take thousands of years. In the meantime, the waste cannot just be thrown in the garbage.

One way to deal with nuclear waste is to recycle it. To do this, scientists take an element called **plutonium** out of nuclear waste. They can use the plutonium to produce electricity in nuclear plants. France recycles much of its nuclear waste in this way. Recycling still makes a small amount of nuclear waste. It cuts down how much waste is made, though.

DID YOU KNOW?

Plutonium can be used to make nuclear weapons. Some people are against recycling nuclear waste because they fear that people might steal plutonium to do this.

The U.S. government has thought about burying nuclear waste under Nevada's Yucca Mountain. However, many people disagree about this plan.

Storing Nuclear Waste

Some nuclear waste is stored at the plants where it was produced. These plants keep nuclear waste for years. However, some plants are starting to run out of room.

People worry that radiation from stored nuclear waste might make those living nearby sick. People also worry that other people might try to steal nuclear waste to make nuclear weapons out of it.

Today, there is more than 50,000 tons (45,360 t) of nuclear waste stored in places around the United States. We need to find new places to put waste, though. This can be hard since the waste must be stored for thousands of years. Few people want nuclear waste stored near them either.

DID YOU KNOW?

Moving nuclear waste can be dangerous. To keep it from spilling, it is moved in holders that are so strong that they will not break. Even fire cannot get through them.

We use electricity to power many things, such as computers and lights. Nuclear power is one of the cleaner ways of making electricity.

Today, much of the electricity that we use in the United States comes from power plants that burn coal. However, supplies of coal will someday run out. Burning coal fills the air with pollution. This can make the air unsafe to breathe. Pollution also gets into Earth's **atmosphere**. This is the layer of gases that circles Earth. Pollution in the atmosphere traps heat near Earth. This changes Earth's weather patterns.

Unlike coal plants, nuclear plants make almost no air pollution. With a piece of fuel the size of a pencil eraser, a nuclear plant can make as much electricity as a coal plant can make with 1 ton (1 t) of coal!

Big Decisions

In the years ahead, we will need cleaner ways to make electricity. Nuclear power plants will likely play a part. However, the waste these plants make raises problems. Also, accidents at nuclear plants can be terrible. After the Chernobyl accident, thousands of people had to leave their homes forever.

Tomorrow's nuclear plants will need strong rules about storing nuclear waste safely. They will also need plans to keep people living nearby safe if accidents happen. People, including those who are kids today, will need to understand nuclear energy and nuclear waste. That way we can make smart decisions about them.

GLOSSARY

atmosphere (AT-muh-sfeer) The gases around an object in space. On Earth this is air.

atoms (A-temz) The smallest parts of elements.

cancer (KAN-ser) A sickness in which cells multiply out of control and do not work properly.

electricity (ih-lek-TRIH-suh-tee) Power that produces light, heat, or movement.

elements (EH-luh-ments) The basic matter of which all things are made.

isotopes (EYE-suh-tohps) Versions of an element with different numbers of neutrons.

nuclear reactor (NOO-klee-ur ree-AK-tur) A machine in which nuclear power is safely released.

nuclear weapons (NOO-klee-ur WEH-punz) Very strong weapons that are sometimes used in times of war.

nucleus (NOO-klee-us) Protons and neutrons joined together in the center of an atom.

plutonium (ploo-TOH-nee-um) A gray element that gives off rays of energy.

radioactive (ray-dee-oh-AK-tiv) Giving off rays of light, heat, or energy.

uranium (yoo-RAY-nee-um) A heavy metallic element that gives off rays of energy.

INDEX

A
atmosphere, 21
atoms, 5, 9, 11, 13, 15

B
bodies, 5, 7, 15

C
cancer, 7, 15

E
electrons, 5
element(s), 9, 17
energy, 5, 9, 11, 13, 22

F
food, 7

I
isotope(s), 9, 15

K
kind(s), 7, 9

M
matter, 5, 7, 9

N
neutrons, 5, 9

nuclear reactor, 9
nucleus, 5

P
people, 7, 11, 13, 15,
    19, 22
plutonium, 17
protons, 5

S
scientists, 5, 9, 17

U
uranium, 9

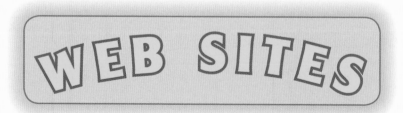

WEB SITES

Due to the changing nature of Internet links, PowerKids Press has developed an online list of Web sites related to the subject of this book. This site is updated regularly. Please use this link to access the list:

www.powerkidslinks.com/pop/nuclear/

24